Flu

ANN O. SQUIRE

Children's Press®
An Imprint of Scholastic Inc.

Content Consultant
Phyllis Meadows, PhD, MSN, RN
Associate Dean for Practice, Clinical Professor, Health Management and Policy
University of Michigan, Ann Arbor, Michigan

Library of Congress Cataloging-in-Publication Data
Names: Squire, Ann, author.
Title: Flu / by Ann O. Squire.
Other titles: True book.
Description: New York, NY : Children's Press, an imprint of Scholastic Inc., [2017] | Series:
   A true book | Includes bibliographical references and index.
Identifiers: LCCN 2015049727| ISBN 9780531228463 (library binding : alk. paper) |
   ISBN 9780531233283 (pbk. : alk. paper)
Subjects: LCSH: Influenza—Juvenile literature. | Influenza—Vaccination—Juvenile literature. |
   Influenza—History—Juvenile literature.
Classification: LCC RC150 .S755 2017 | DDC 616.2/03—dc23
LC record available at http://lccn.loc.gov/2015049727

Front cover: A sick child
Back cover: Flu viruses

Find the Truth!

Everything you are about to read is true *except* for one of the sentences on this page.

Which one is **TRUE**?

T or F If you've had a flu shot, you never need to get another one.

T or F The flu spreads from person to person very easily.

Find the answers in this book.

3

Contents

THE BIG TRUTH!

Influenza
vaccine

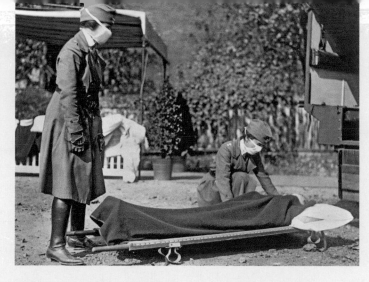

The 1918 flu
pandemic

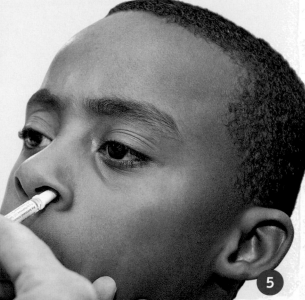

A patient receiving
a nasal spray flu
vaccine

CHAPTER 1

Is It the Flu?

Mary had never felt so sick in her life. She normally jumped out of bed when her mom came to wake her up each morning. But today Mary could barely move. Her body ached, her throat was sore, and she felt cold even though she was covered in blankets. Her mom had taken her temperature, and it was several degrees above normal. Mary would stay home from school today.

People with the flu often have a temperature above 100 degrees Fahrenheit (38 degrees Celsius).

Worse Than a Cold

Mary had had colds before, but this felt different.
When she had a cold, her nose was stuffy and
runny. Aside from that, she didn't feel that bad.
Today seemed completely different. Mary's mom
thought so, too. After taking her daughter's
temperature, she placed a call to the doctor to ask
his advice.

If you have
a fever, it is
better to stay
home and
rest instead
of going to
school.

It's a good idea to see your doctor if you experience flu symptoms.

The doctor had received several calls that morning from patients with similar **symptoms**. Based on these symptoms and the time of year, he suspected that his patients had the flu. Mary's mom asked if she should bring her daughter in. The doctor said no. While tests can indicate whether a person has the flu, they are not always needed.

Based on Mary's symptoms, the doctor knew without seeing her that she had the flu. He recommended that she stay home for the next few days, drink lots of liquids, and take pain relievers and **decongestants** if she needed them. He predicted that she would start to feel better in a couple of days.

Warm drinks such as tea can help you feel better when you have the flu.

Cold or Flu?

It's sometimes difficult to tell if you have the flu or a bad cold. Both are **viruses**. Their symptoms can affect your nose, sinuses, throat, and lungs. These symptoms can be similar. However, a cold is usually milder than the flu. Your nose may be stuffy, but you usually don't have symptoms such as a fever or body aches. If you're feeling really sick, always call a doctor for advice.

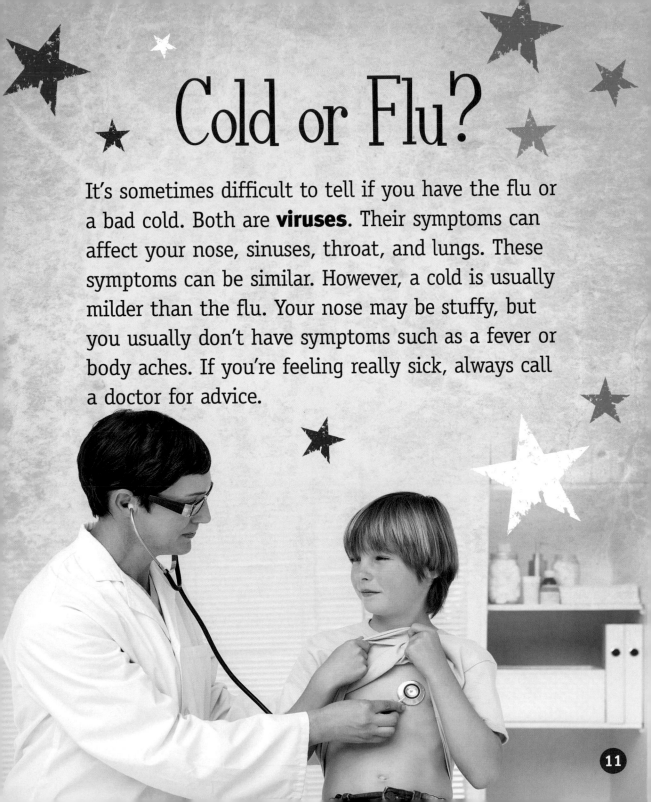

CHAPTER 2

What Is the Flu?

The flu, also called influenza, is a virus that targets your respiratory system—your nose, throat, and lungs. The flu is very **contagious**. When an infected person coughs or sneezes, tiny droplets of fluid carrying the virus fly into the air. If you breathe these droplets in or they land in your mouth or eyes, you might get sick.

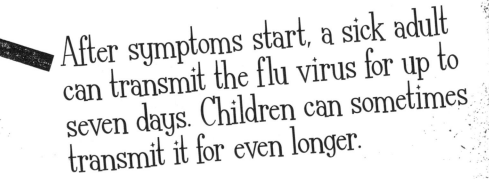

After symptoms start, a sick adult can transmit the flu virus for up to seven days. Children can sometimes transmit it for even longer.

Objects that many people touch, such as doorknobs, are common places to pick up germs.

How the Flu Makes You Sick

The flu can also be transmitted when an infected person touches something like a doorknob or handrail. Healthy people might touch that same surface. If they touch their nose, eyes, or mouth, the virus can enter their body and infect them. Flu symptoms can take one to four days to appear, so people can pass on the virus even before they know they are sick.

When the flu virus enters the body, it binds to the surface of cells in the nose, throat, and lungs. The virus takes over the function of the cells. It begins to make many copies of itself. Soon the virus enters the bloodstream and begins to spread. The respiratory system becomes irritated and swollen. Other symptoms, such as fever, also begin to appear.

The flu virus is so small that it can be seen only with a microscope.

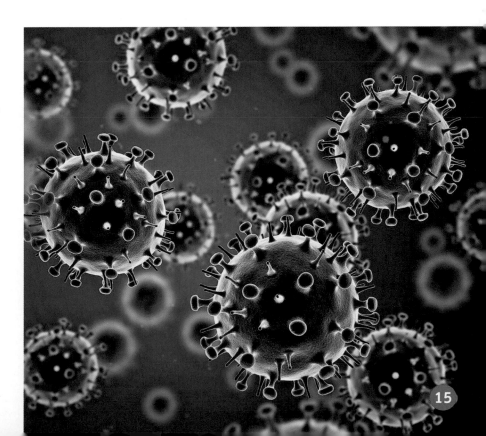

The Immune System

Your body has a way of fighting back when it is attacked by a virus. Your immune system protects your body against disease and infection. It springs into action when it detects a virus or some other invader. The immune system creates **antibodies**. Antibodies prevent viruses from reproducing or mark them so the body can recognize and destroy them.

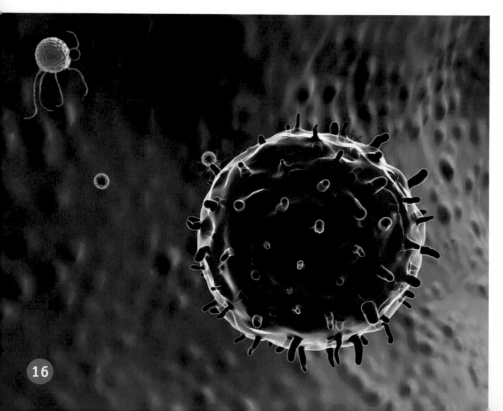

Antibodies (green) mark a virus (purple) as a threat.

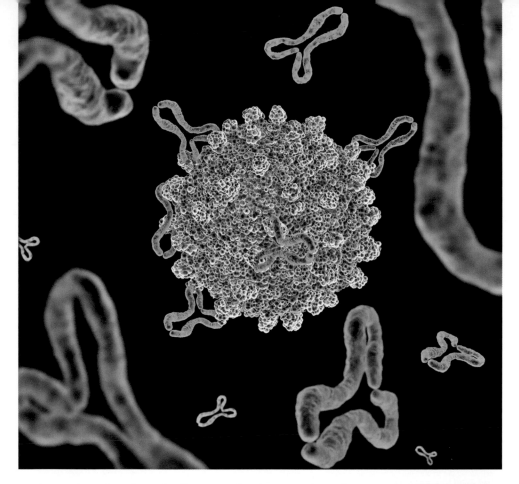

Y-shaped antibodies (yellow, in the image above) surround a virus.

After your immune system has gotten rid of a virus, special cells hold on to an "image" of that virus. If it tries to attack the body again, the immune system can immediately begin fighting it. When this happens, we are said to be immune to the effects of the virus. It can no longer make us sick.

But why can we get the flu over and over again? Shouldn't we become immune after the first time? Don't blame your immune system. Many viruses, including the flu, are very good at **mutating**, or changing themselves as they reproduce. When a virus changes even a little bit, your immune system no longer recognizes it. The virus is able to make you sick again.

No matter how many times you get the flu, you are always at risk of catching a mutated version later on.

Children and senior citizens must be particularly careful about avoiding the flu.

A Greater Risk

People with weakened immune systems are more likely than others to become very ill or even die when they have the flu. For example, the immune systems of young children are not yet fully developed. Senior citizens and people with medical conditions such as asthma or diabetes also have weak immune systems. This places them at greater risk for flu complications.

Getting a Flu Shot

You may have heard about flu shots. Maybe you have even received one from your doctor. The flu shot is a **vaccine**. A vaccine is a substance that contains small amounts of a virus or other illness. When a vaccine is injected into your body, your immune system uses it to develop antibodies. This means your body will be ready to fight off an infection if you are ever exposed to the virus. You will not get sick.

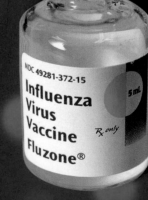

NDC 49281-372-15

Influenza
Virus
Vaccine
Fluzone®

5 mL

Rx only

Before the invention of the flu vaccine, the flu affected far more people than it does today. The first working flu vaccine was developed in the 1940s. It was given to soldiers fighting in World War II.

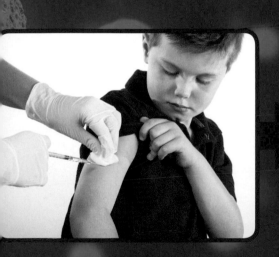

There are many different flu viruses. A single shot cannot protect you from all of them. Each year, doctors and public health officials identify three or four flu viruses that they expect to be particularly dangerous that year. Then they develop a vaccine to protect against those viruses. Because flu viruses can change quickly, the flu shot you get one year may be very different from the one you got the previous year. This is why it's important to get a flu shot every year.

Flu viruses can affect pets and other animals just as they do humans.

CHAPTER 3

Not Just for People

Humans are not the only ones who suffer from the flu. Specialized flu viruses can affect animals as well. Ferrets, pigs, horses, ducks, chickens, dogs, and cats are just some of the nonhuman species that can become infected. The flu works in animals much as it does in people, targeting the respiratory system and causing coughing, fever, and a runny nose.

 No human has ever reported catching canine (dog) flu.

A Danger to Animals

Dogs and cats that catch the flu usually recover with no lasting problems. But some species are not so lucky. Equine flu, or horse flu, is highly contagious. If one horse in a herd becomes infected, the virus usually spreads rapidly and causes lasting damage. Humans cannot catch equine flu. However, some other types of animal flu can be shared between species.

Because the flu affects the respiratory system and makes it hard to breathe, it can affect a horse's ability to run quickly.

Because chickens and other farm birds are usually kept in close quarters, flu can spread very quickly among them.

These are a great concern among public health officials. One of the most dangerous is avian flu, or bird flu. Avian flu occurs naturally in wild ducks, geese, and other waterbirds. If infected wild birds come into contact with domestic birds, such as chickens or turkeys, the virus can spread quickly. Some forms of avian flu cause only minor symptoms. Others can cause serious illness and death.

Humans who work closely with birds are sometimes at risk of catching the flu from them.

From Birds to Humans

It is rare for people to become infected with avian flu, but it has happened among people who have had contact with sick or dead birds. Humans have no antibodies for this type of flu, so they can become very sick. Since 2005, more than 800 cases of humans with avian flu have been reported. More than half of those people died of the illness.

Even if a person contracts avian flu, he or she cannot pass it on to anyone else. The virus does not spread among people. We've learned, though, that flu viruses can change rapidly and adapt to new conditions. Scientists speculate that avian flu could one day mutate and develop the ability to spread from person to person.

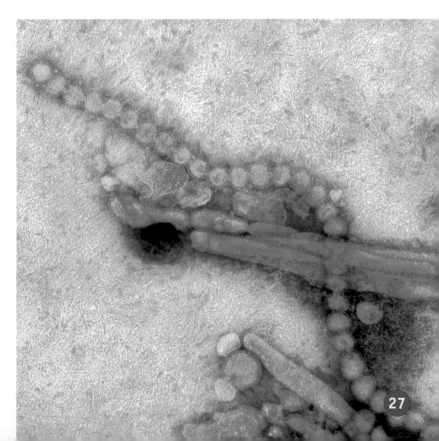

This microscopic image shows one type of avian flu that infected several people in China in 2013 and eventually spread to the nation of Malaysia.

CHAPTER 4

A Worldwide Tragedy

A few cases of the flu might not seem like a big deal. However, the flu is highly contagious. One sick person might spread the illness to several others. Those others spread the sickness to even more people. Some people might travel and infect people living far away. Before long, the flu has spread around the world.

If someone with the flu visits a crowded airport, the virus can quickly spread around the world.

The Spread of Sickness

When a sickness affects many people in a small area, it is called an outbreak. If it suddenly spreads to a larger area, the problem is known as an **epidemic**. Worst of all is a **pandemic**. This is a situation when a disease spreads to several countries or possibly even the whole world.

Certain types of viruses are particularly dangerous, and researchers must wear protective clothing when experimenting with them.

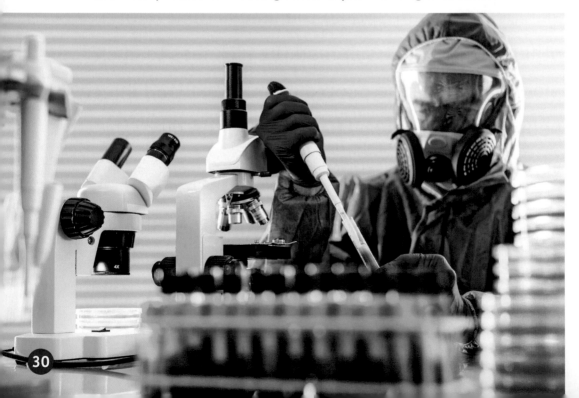

The Flu Pandemic of 1918

The world breathed a sigh of relief when World War I ended in 1918. Millions of people had been injured or killed during the war. But just when people thought they could relax and return

World War I was one of the deadliest wars in history.

to their normal lives, another threat emerged: a deadly flu pandemic that ended up claiming more lives than the war.

The virus first appeared in the United States in January 1918, when soldiers at a base in Kansas began to fall ill with the flu. This flu was more serious than any officials had seen before. They alerted the U.S. Public Health Service (PHS) that they were dealing with cases of severe influenza. Within several months, the flu had spread around the globe.

Timeline of Flu Pandemics

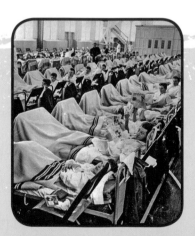

1918–1919

Around 50 million people die in the "Spanish Flu" pandemic.

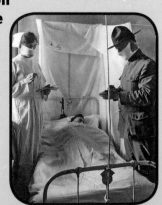

1957–1958

A flu pandemic begins in Asia and spreads to the United States, killing tens of thousands.

Not Enough Doctors

Many U.S. medical workers were overseas treating injured soldiers. As a result, some communities had no doctors or nurses available to treat flu patients. The PHS had only 700 officers on duty. This was not nearly enough to deal with the fast-spreading virus. Even when PHS doctors and nurses were there to help, they often fell ill themselves before they could treat patients.

1968–1969

A flu pandemic begins in Hong Kong, killing as many as 4 million people worldwide.

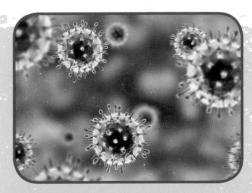

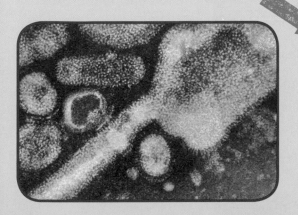

2009–2010

The H1N1 flu virus affects between 43 and 89 million people worldwide in a single wave.

A National Disaster

Unlike most flu outbreaks, which are particularly dangerous for children and the elderly, the 1918 flu epidemic struck people of all ages. In some places, entire families were wiped out. Philadelphia was hit particularly hard. Adults got sick and died. Many children were orphaned. So many children lost their parents that the city's Bureau of Child Hygiene was overwhelmed and could not care for all of them.

Red Cross nurses demonstrate proper treatment at an emergency ambulance station during the 1918 epidemic.

The Spanish Flu

World War I was a terrifying period in history. To avoid scaring people further, newspapers did not print stories about the flu pandemic in countries involved in the war. Spain was not part of the war, so the press felt free to cover the pandemic there. People got the impression that Spain had been hit especially hard. They began calling the pandemic the "Spanish Flu."

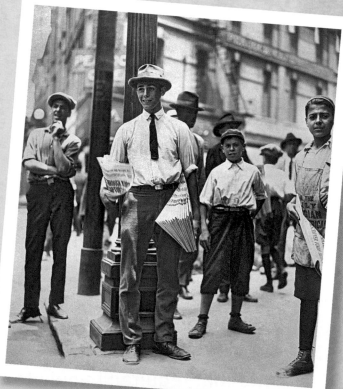

Informational posters helped people learn how to avoid catching or spreading illness in 1918.

INFLUENZA

FREQUENTLY COMPLICATED WITH

PNEUMONIA

IS PREVALENT AT THIS TIME THROUGHOUT AMERICA.

THIS THEATRE IS CO-OPERATING WITH THE DEPARTMENT OF HEALTH.

YOU MUST DO THE SAME

IF YOU HAVE A COLD AND ARE COUGHING AND SNEEZING. DO NOT ENTER THIS THEATRE

GO HOME AND GO TO BED UNTIL YOU ARE WELL

Coughing, Sneezing or Spitting Will Not Be Permitted In The Theatre. In case you must cough or Sneeze, do so in your own handkerchief, and if the Coughing or Sneezing Persists Leave The Theatre At Once.

This Theatre has agreed to co-operate with the Department Of Health in disseminating the truth about Influenza, and thus serve a great educational purpose.

HELP US TO KEEP CHICAGO THE HEALTHIEST CITY IN THE WORLD

JOHN DILL ROBERTSON
COMMISSIONER OF HEALTH

Cities and towns took drastic measures to keep the flu from spreading. **Quarantines** were put in place. Schools, theaters, restaurants, and even churches were closed. Public health announcements urged people not to sneeze, spit, or cough in public. Some communities passed laws that required people to wear masks when out in public.

No Protection

At the time, no one knew that the flu was caused by a virus or that masks offered almost no protection. With no effective way to prevent the flu, the pandemic continued to spread. By the time it ended in spring 1919, nearly 675,000 Americans had died. An estimated 50 million people died worldwide. In fact, nearly as many people died in the flu pandemic as in World War I. Most families were affected in some way.

A British nurse shows a soldier how to wear a face mask during the 1918 pandemic.

You should be
especially careful
about catching the flu
during the winter.

Preventing the Flu

Although you can catch the flu any time of year, most people become infected during winter. The peak of the flu season usually happens between December and February. Part of the reason for this is that people spend more time indoors during cold weather. This means they are more likely to be in close contact with others. The flu spreads easily from person to person in these situations.

An estimated 5 to 20 percent of the U.S. population catches the flu in a single flu season.

Staying Healthy

Fortunately, there are many ways of preventing the flu. The number one recommendation made by doctors is to get a flu shot by October each year. This gives the vaccine time to start working and protect you against the kinds of flu virus that health officials expect to be most dangerous that year. Most flu vaccines are given as shots. Some types are available as a nasal spray.

A nasal spray is a quick and easy way to get a flu vaccination.

Be sure to wash your hands well and dry them completely afterward.

If you have the flu, doctors recommend that you stay home for at least 24 hours after your fever is gone.

You can also protect yourself and others by practicing good health habits. Washing your hands often with soap and warm water, using hand sanitizer, and avoiding contact with sick people will all reduce your chances of getting the flu. If you are already sick, you can avoid spreading the virus by staying home from school and taking a break from activities with other people.

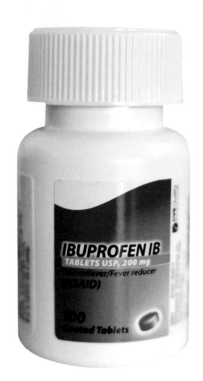

Sometimes a simple pain reliever such as ibuprofen is all it takes to make you feel better when you have the flu.

Getting Better

For most people, getting over the flu is a simple matter. A few days of rest and plenty of fluids are usually all that is necessary. But if your symptoms are very severe, be sure to see your doctor. He or she may prescribe medicine to reduce your symptoms, make you get better more quickly, and keep your flu from developing into a more serious condition.

Increased Risk of Flu Complications

The flu can cause major problems for people with the following medical conditions:

- Asthma, diabetes, or other chronic diseases
- Heart disease, kidney, or liver disorders
- Chronic lung disease
- Weakened immune system due to disease (such as HIV or cancer) or medication (such as steroids)

People with these conditions should see a doctor immediately if they catch the flu. With rest and proper treatment, they can beat the illness and return to normal life soon! ★

If you have asthma, the flu can be especially dangerous.

True Statistics

Number of children under 5 in the United States who are hospitalized each year with complications from the flu: 20,000

Percent of total flu-related deaths represented by people 65 and older: 80 to 90

Time it takes after receiving a flu shot for protection to begin: 2 weeks

Percent of the world's population infected during the 1918–1919 flu epidemic: More than 30

Estimated number of Americans who died in the 1918–1919 flu epidemic: 675,000

Number of people worldwide who died in the 1918–1919 flu epidemic: About 50 million

Did you find the truth?

(F) If you've had a flu shot, you never need to get another one.

(T) The flu spreads from person to person very easily.

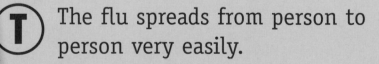
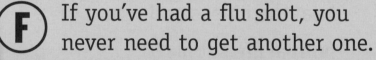

Resources

Books

Cunningham, Kevin. *Pandemics.* New York: Children's Press, 2012.

Rudolph, Jessica. *The Flu of 1918: Millions Dead Worldwide!* New York: Bearport Publishing, 2011.

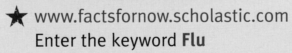

Visit this Scholastic Web site for more information on flu:
★ www.factsfornow.scholastic.com
Enter the keyword **Flu**

Important Words

antibodies (AN-ti-bah-deez) substances the blood produces to stop an infection that has entered the body

contagious (kuhn-TAY-juhs) spread by direct or indirect contact with an infected person or animal

decongestants (dee-kuhn-JES-tuhnts) medicines or treatments that make breathing easier for a person with a cold or infection

epidemic (ep-uh-DEM-ik) an infectious disease present in a large number of people at the same time

mutating (MYOO-tay-ting) changing into something different

pandemic (pan-DEM-ik) an outbreak of a disease that affects a very large region or the whole world

quarantines (KWOR-uhn-teenz) situations in which people, animals, or plants are kept away from others for a period of time to stop a disease from spreading

symptoms (SIMP-tuhmz) signs of an illness

vaccine (vak-SEEN) a substance containing dead, weakened, or living organisms that can be injected or taken orally; a vaccine causes a person to produce antibodies that protect him or her from the disease caused by the organisms

viruses (VYE-ruhs-iz) tiny organisms that can reproduce and grow only when inside living cells

Index

Page numbers in **bold** indicate illustrations.

About the Author

Ann O. Squire is a psychologist and an animal behaviorist. Before becoming a writer, she studied the behavior of rats, tropical fish in the Caribbean, and electric fish from central Africa. Her favorite part of being a writer is the chance to learn as much as she can about all sorts of topics. In addition to *Flu* and books on other health topics, Dr. Squire has written about many different animals, from lemmings to leopards and cicadas to cheetahs. She lives in Asheville, North Carolina.